ISBN: 978-1-7345026-3-3
LCCN: 2020909370

Cover design: Bonnie Lemaire
Editor: Candice L. Davis

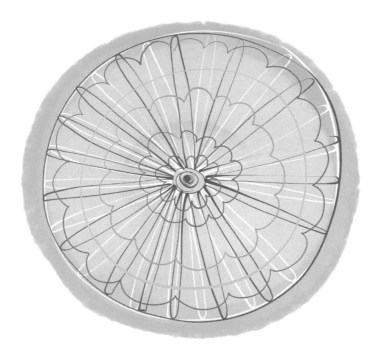

This book was inspired by the countless students who have passed through my classroom. Your resilience, fortitude, and self-determination inspire me more than you know. I love each of you.

To my children, may you always know that you are deeply loved.

To Gloria (Duck) Holloway, may your love live on in the stories and memories of your grandchildren. We love and miss you.

Dear Parents,

Your child's brain rapidly develops between conception and age six. In fact, most of your child's brain development will occur in the earliest parts of life. It's never too early (or too late) to start talking to your child about the developing brain and how it works. A nutritious diet and positive experiences and relationships are crucial for healthy brain development. By reading to, playing with, and introducing mindfulness strategies to your child, you can help him or her develop healthy, brain-boosting habits that last a lifetime. This journal is filled with 5-minute mindfulness activities kids can complete with or without an adult. However, I encourage you to work through this journal with your child and to model these strategies every day.

Each week, your child will be introduced to a new breathing tool. I encourage you to engage with them in these breathing activities each day. I suggest taking 3-5 minutes to meditate together. I typically do this with my girls before bedtime to help with the transition, but you can do this at any time and in any place that best suits your family.

This journal begins by introducing a bit of brain science and terminology. We begin with the **amygdala** (uh-mig-duh-luh), the brain's security guard, where "big feelings" like flight, flight, and freeze live. Sometimes this part of our brain roars when we are scared, angry, or frustrated, or when we think we need to protect ourselves. The **prefrontal cortex**, where logical thinking and emotional regulation live, is our brain's problem solver. These strategies are designed to help boost our emotional regulation. Lastly, the **hippocampus**, is our brain's memory keeper. It stores information. Toxic stress can cause our brains to not hold on to our memories. Mindfulness helps with that, too!

Children can "flip their lids" when they're unable to regulate their emotions. Meditation, breathing, and yoga are mindfulness tools that help kids think before they act. These tools can help to rescue us from "getting stuck in the mud." They help us to move from a fixed to a growth mindset.

For additional information, activities, and resources, check out the best-selling book, *The Mindfulness Room*, and rethinkingresiliency.com.

Mindfulness Essentials

- **FIND A BUDDY**-PARENTS, I ENCOURAGE YOU TO PARTICIPATE IN THESE JOURNAL PROMPTS AND EXERCISES WITH YOUR CHILD. IT MAY HELP YOUR CHILD TO TALK TO YOU ABOUT THEIR EXPERIENCE AND IT WILL ENCOURAGE CONSISTENCY.

- **JOURNAL**-AFTER YOUR CHILD COMPLETES THEIR BREATHWORK OR MEDITATION ACTIVITIES, THEY SHOULD TAKE TIME TO NOTE HOW THEY FEEL IN THE JOURNAL. THEY SHOULD WRITE ABOUT GOOD AND DIFFICULT MOMENTS IN THEIR DAY.

- **MAKE TIME TO MEDITATE**-LIFE IS BUSY! THE KEY TO BUILDING A MINDFUL PRACTICE IS TO MAKE IT A PRIORITY. SET ASIDE A SPECIFIC TIME TO PRACTICE. START WITH FIVE MINUTES AND GROW FROM THERE.

- **CREATE A COZY SPACE**-YOUR CHILD CAN PRACTICE ANYWHERE: IN THEIR BEDROOM, IN THEIR BACKYARD, OR EVEN IN THEIR BATHROOM. TRY TO CREATE A DEDICATED SPACE IN YOUR HOME FOR MINDFULNESS.

- **BE CONSISTENT**-JUST KEEP SHOWING UP AND PRACTICING EVERY DAY! LIKE ANYTHING ELSE, THE MORE THEY PRACTICE, THE STRONGER THEIR BRAIN WILL BE.

- **BE KIND TO YOURSELF**-CONGRATULATE YOURSELF FOR SHOWING UP! REMIND YOURSELF THAT SHOWING UP IS THE FIRST STEP TO DEVELOPING A PRACTICE. YOU'RE DOING GREAT!

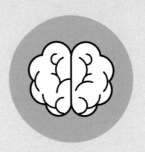

BRAIN POWER

WORDS TO KNOW

Amygdala

You have two amygdala in your brain. They are almond shaped and just above your ear. They are your brain's security guards and tell you when you are not safe. Sometimes this makes you "flip your lid". The feelings of fight, flight, and freeze are stored here.

Prefrontal cortex

Your prefrontal cortex is located in the front of your brain. It is your brain's problem solver. It helps you make good decisions, guide your behavior, and helps keep you organized.

Hippocampus

The hippocampus is located deep inside of your brain. It is your brain's memory keeper and stores information.

Name: _____   Date: _____

What does it mean?

Draw a line between the columns to match the word with its meaning.

amygdala ○   ○ Your brain's memory keeper

hippocampus ○   ○ Your brain's security guard

prefrontal
cortex ○   ○ Your brain's problem solver

don't get stuck in the mud

WE ALL HAVE BIG FEELINGS
SADNESS
ANGER
FEAR
LONELINESS
FRUSTRATION

BUT WE DON'T WANT TO GET STUCK IN THOSE FEELINGS. I CALL
THAT BEING STUCK IN THE MUD.

SOMETIMES OUR BRAINS TELL US TO FLIP OUR LIDS, TO BE
SCARED, TO RUN AWAY, OR TO GET STUCK IN THOSE BIG
FEELINGS, EVEN WHEN WE ARE SAFE.

THIS IS OUR AMYGDALA WORKING TOO HARD.

IN THIS JOURNAL, YOU WILL LEARN NEW TOOLS TO HELP YOU
SO YOU DON'T GET STUCK IN THE MUD. THESE TOOLS WILL HELP
MAKE YOUR BRAIN STRONGER.

Name: Date:

Building my amygdala toolkit

A part of building your amygdala tool kit is identifying strategies you can use when you feel "stuck in the mud."
Cut the words on this page along the dotted lines.
Then, paste them into the correct columns to create your toolkit.
You can also write in your own strategies in the blank spaces.

MIND	BODY	ENVIRONMENT

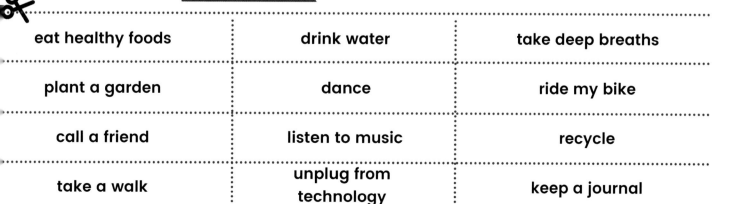

eat healthy foods	drink water	take deep breaths
plant a garden	dance	ride my bike
call a friend	listen to music	recycle
take a walk	unplug from technology	keep a journal

Dream big and make it

happen!

Set your intention

- [ ] DRINK 8 GLASSES OF WATER A DAY
- [ ] UNPLUG FROM SOCIAL MEDIA AND VIDEO GAMES FOR 24 HOURS
- [ ] SIT IN THE SUNSHINE
- [ ] TAKE A WALK
- [ ] CREATE A GRATITUDE JAR
- [ ] 3 MINUTES OF BELLY BREATHING
- [ ] TAKE A DANCE BREAK
- [ ] LISTEN TO YOUR FAVORITE SONG
- [ ] CALL A FRIEND
- [ ] VISIT A FAMILY MEMBER
- [ ] TAKE A BIKE RIDE
- [ ] TAKE A WARM BATH
- [ ] CUDDLE A PET
- [ ] TRY SOMETHING NEW
- [ ] READ A GOOD BOOK

Name: Date:

WHAT HAPPENED TODAY?

Write about something that made you happy today.

Belly Breathing
Diaphragmatic breathing
(3 minutes)

You are always breathing. Though your breath flows in and out it's always with you. You can control your breathing and return to it at any time. Remember you are working to make your brain stronger!

Steps

1. Get into a comfy position. You can stand, sit, or lie down. You may use a pillow, mat, cushion, or chair, just make sure you're comfortable.
2. Close your eyes if that feels okay, or you can look at the tip of your nose. Allow yourself to relax.
3. Bring your attention and awareness to your belly. As you breathe in, inflate your belly like a beach ball or balloon.
4. Relax your tummy on your exhale, when you breathe out.
5. You can also place a stuffy or doll on your belly and pretend it's riding a wave, going up and down.
6. Try this by yourself or with a buddy for three minutes.

NAME: _____ DATE: _____

WHAT'S MY SUPERPOWER?

If you became a superhero for a day, who would you be?
What would be your superpower(s)?

_____

_____

_____

_____

_____

_____

_____

_____

_____

WHAT HAPPENED TODAY?

Write about something that frustrated you today.
What did you do about it?

Name: _____   Date: _____

WHO AM I?

Use the space below to draw a self-portrait. On the left side, draw how you look
on the outside. On the right side, draw how you feel on the inside.
Don't forget to talk about it with your journal buddy if you want.
Color your creation when you're done!

Name: Date:

WHAT HAPPENED TODAY?

Write about something that happened today
that you would like you remember.

GROWING YOUR AWARENESS

During the daytime, find a quiet space outside or near a window. Take a few deep, cleansing breaths, close your eyes if you want, and bring awareness to your environment. Then, draw what you hear and smell. Come back to the same spot at night and draw what you hear and smell. Compare your drawings. Write down things that are the same and things that are different.

Day	Night

☆ ☆ SIMILARITIES ☆ ☆

_____
_____
_____

☆ ☆ DIFFERENCES ☆ ☆

_____
_____
_____

Name:

Date:

WHAT ARE YOU THANKFUL FOR TODAY?

Write about three things that you are thankful for today.

May you be happy.
May you be healthy.
May you be safe.
May you be loved.

Focus on your

breath...

Set your intention

CHECK THREE THINGS YOU WILL DO THIS
WEEK TO BE MORE MINDFUL.
BE INTENTIONAL.

- [ ] DRINK 8 GLASSES OF WATER A DAY
- [ ] UNPLUG FROM SOCIAL MEDIA AND VIDEO GAMES FOR 24 HOURS
- [ ] SIT IN THE SUNSHINE
- [ ] TAKE A WALK
- [ ] CREATE A GRATITUDE JAR
- [ ] 3 MINUTES OF BELLY BREATHING
- [ ] TAKE A DANCE BREAK
- [ ] LISTEN TO YOUR FAVORITE SONG
- [ ] CALL A FRIEND
- [ ] VISIT A FAMILY MEMBER
- [ ] TAKE A BIKE RIDE
- [ ] TAKE A WARM BATH
- [ ] CUDDLE A PET
- [ ] TRY SOMETHING NEW
- [ ] READ A GOOD BOOK

Lion's Breath
Simhasana
(3 minutes)

YOU ARE ALWAYS BREATHING. THOUGH YOUR BREATH FLOWS IN AND OUT IT'S ALWAYS WITH YOU. YOU CAN CONTROL YOUR BREATHING AND RETURN TO IT AT ANY TIME. REMEMBER YOU ARE WORKING TO MAKE YOUR BRAIN STRONGER!

STEPS

1. GET INTO A COMFY POSITION. I RECOMMEND SITTING ON A CUSHION, A CHAIR, OR CRISS-CROSS-APPLESAUCE ON THE FLOOR. JUST MAKE SURE YOU'RE COMFORTABLE.
2. TAKE A DEEP CLEANSING BREATH.
3. LOOK UP AT THE CEILING.
4. OPEN YOUR MOUTH AS WIDE AS YOU CAN.
5. STICK YOUR TONGUE OUT AS FAR AS IT WILL GO, CURLING YOUR TONGUE DOWNWARD.
6. EXHALE FORCEFULLY WHILE MAKING A "HAAAA" SOUND.
7. TRY THIS BY YOURSELF OR WITH A BUDDY FOR THREE MINUTES.

What's Your Mood?

How are you feeling today? Sad? Happy? Excited? Mad? Frustrated? Joyful?

Draw a self-portrait of how you feel today on the image below.

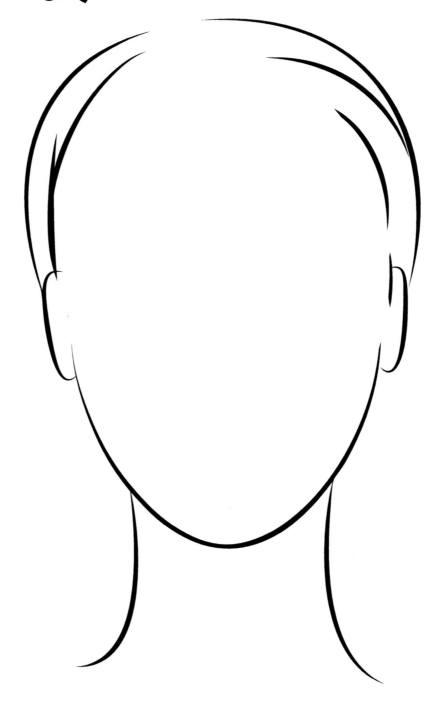

name: _____

WHAT HAPPENED TODAY?

Write about something that made you happy today.

YOU ARE AWESOME

MINDFUL MOVEMENT

Notice the natural rhythm of your breath.
Jump rope for one minute and notice any changes to your breathing.
Notice how your breath feels. Hot? Cold? Fast? Slow?
Write your observations below.

Name: Date:

WHAT HAPPENED TODAY?

Write about something that frustrated you today.
What did you do about it?

WHAT ARE YOU THANKFUL FOR TODAY?

Write about three things that you are thankful for today.

GROWING YOUR AWARENESS

During the daytime, find a quiet space outside or near a window. Take a few deep, cleansing breaths, close your eyes if you want, and bring awareness to your environment. Then, draw what you hear and smell. Come back to the same spot at night and draw what you hear and smell. Compare your drawings.
Write down things that are the same and things that are different.

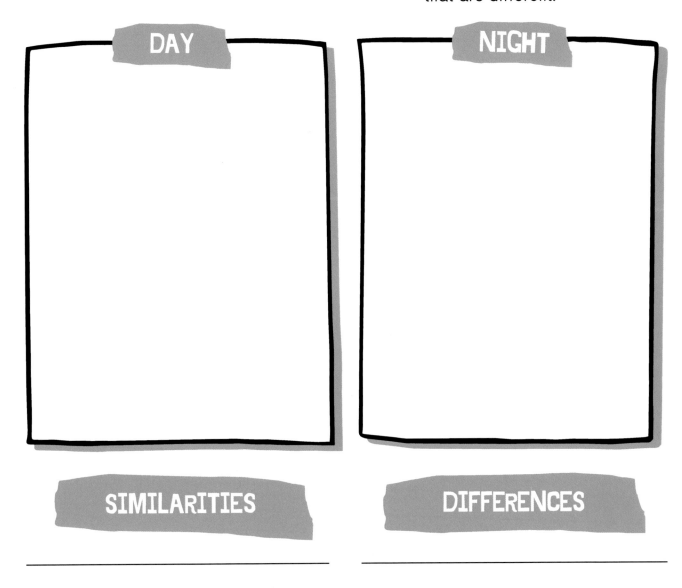

DAY

NIGHT

SIMILARITIES

_____
_____
_____
_____
_____

DIFFERENCES

_____
_____
_____
_____
_____

Name: Date:

WHAT HAPPENED TODAY?

Write about something that happened today
that you would like you remember.

Set your intention

CHECK THREE THINGS YOU WILL DO THIS
WEEK TO BE MORE MINDFUL.
BE INTENTIONAL.

- [ ] DRINK 8 GLASSES OF WATER A DAY
- [ ] UNPLUG FROM SOCIAL MEDIA AND VIDEO GAMES FOR 24 HOURS
- [ ] SIT IN THE SUNSHINE
- [ ] TAKE A WALK
- [ ] CREATE A GRATITUDE JAR
- [ ] 3 MINUTES OF BELLY BREATHING
- [ ] TAKE A DANCE BREAK
- [ ] LISTEN TO YOUR FAVORITE SONG
- [ ] CALL A FRIEND
- [ ] VISIT A FAMILY MEMBER
- [ ] TAKE A BIKE RIDE
- [ ] TAKE A WARM BATH
- [ ] CUDDLE A PET
- [ ] TRY SOMETHING NEW
- [ ] READ A GOOD BOOK

Ocean breath
Ujjayi Pranayama
(3 minutes)

YOU ARE ALWAYS BREATHING. THOUGH YOUR BREATH FLOWS IN AND OUT IT'S ALWAYS WITH YOU. YOU CAN CONTROL YOUR BREATHING AND RETURN TO IT AT ANY TIME. OCEAN BREATH HELPS YOU FOCUS, RELAX, AND MAKES YOUR LUNGS STRONGER.

STEPS

1. COME INTO A COMFY SEATED POSITION. THIS CAN BE IN A CHAIR, ON A MAT, OR ON A CUSHION. JUST MAKE SURE YOU ARE COMFORTABLE.
2. GRAB A MIRROR OR GLASS AND FOG IT UP WITH YOUR BREATH.
3. CALL YOUR ATTENTION TO THE HISSING SOUND THAT YOUR BREATH MAKES. IT SOUNDS SORT OF LIKE THE OCEAN. DO YOU HEAR IT?
4. CLOSE YOUR MOUTH AND SEE IF YOU CAN MAKE THE SAME SOUND AND SENSATION ON BOTH THE INHALE AND EXHALE.

THIS BREATHING PATTERN HELPS TO CALM THE BODY'S FIGHT-OR-FLIGHT RESPONSE. TRY BREATHING THIS WAY FOR THREE MINUTES.

What's Your Mood?

How are you feeling today? Sad? Happy? Excited? Mad? Frustrated? Joyful?

Draw a self-portrait of how you feel today on the image below.

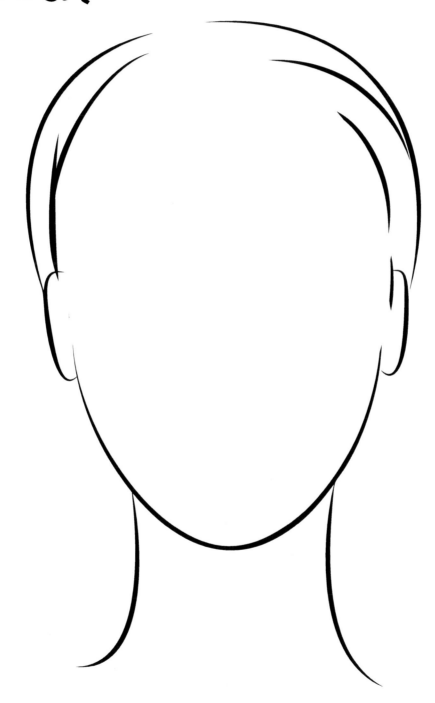

name: _____

WHAT HAPPENED TODAY?

Write about something that made you happy today.

50 AFFIRMATIONS

Circle ten statements that best describe you.
Create your own affirmation statements on the next page.

I am brave.	I am worthy.
I am happy.	I am a superstar.
I am proud.	I am dependable.
I am kind.	I am trustworthy.
I am funny.	I am amazing.
I am honest.	I am a giver.
I am thankful.	I am consistent.
I am silly.	I am capable.
I am in control of my feelings.	I am a leader.
I am smart.	I am hardworking.
I am helpful.	I am wise.
I am a good friend.	I am powerful.
I am curious.	I am open-minded.
I am resilient.	I am my own superhero.
I am talented.	I am one of a kind.
I am a problem solver.	I am perfect just the way I am.
I am a winner.	I am complete.
I am joyous.	I am quick-witted.
I am peaceful.	I am assertive.
I am safe.	I am a thinker.
I am healthy.	I am true to myself.
I am confident.	I am deserving.
I am beautiful.	I am loved.
I am strong.	I am mindful.
I am free.	I am grateful.

Name: **Date:**

I AM.....

List five affirmation statements below.

Name: Date:

WHAT HAPPENED TODAY?

Write about something that frustrated you today.
What did you do about it?

WHAT ARE YOU THANKFUL FOR TODAY?

Write about three things that you are thankful for today.

WHAT HAPPENED TODAY?

Write about something that happened today
that you would like you remember.

I am happy.
I am kind.
I am peace.

Set your intention

CHECK THREE THINGS YOU WILL DO THIS WEEK TO BE MORE MINDFUL. BE INTENTIONAL.

- [ ] DRINK 8 GLASSES OF WATER A DAY
- [ ] UNPLUG FROM SOCIAL MEDIA AND VIDEO GAMES FOR 24 HOURS
- [ ] SIT IN THE SUNSHINE
- [ ] TAKE A WALK
- [ ] CREATE A GRATITUDE JAR
- [ ] 3 MINUTES OF BELLY BREATHING
- [ ] TAKE A DANCE BREAK
- [ ] LISTEN TO YOUR FAVORITE SONG
- [ ] CALL A FRIEND
- [ ] VISIT A FAMILY MEMBER
- [ ] TAKE A BIKE RIDE
- [ ] TAKE A WARM BATH
- [ ] CUDDLE A PET
- [ ] TRY SOMETHING NEW
- [ ] READ A GOOD BOOK

Dinosaur Feet
Walking Meditation
(3 minutes)

YOU ARE ALWAYS BREATHING. THOUGH YOUR BREATH FLOWS IN AND OUT IT'S ALWAYS WITH YOU. YOU CAN PRACTICE DINOSAUR FEET INSIDE OR OUTSIDE. HAVE FUN!

STEPS

1. BRING YOUR AWARENESS TO YOUR FEET.
2. CLOSE YOUR EYES AND WALK SLOWLY LEFT TO RIGHT, ROLLING YOUR ANKLES AND WIGGLING YOUR TOES.
3. SLOWLY WALK IN PLACE AND FOCUS ON THE SENSATIONS IN YOUR FEET.
4. SLOWLY LIFT YOUR FEET AND TAKE BIG STEPS ACROSS THE ROOM OR SPACE.
5. DO THIS IN SILENCE.
6. YOU CAN ALSO EXTEND OR ROLL YOUR NECK WHILE WALKING SLOWLY ACROSS THE ROOM OR SPACE.

TRY ALSO DRAWING YOUR ATTENTION TO THINGS IN YOUR ENVIRONMENT SUCH AS SOUNDS, ANIMALS, OR OTHER SENSATIONS IN YOUR BODY.

Name: Date:

WHAT HAPPENED TODAY?

Write about something that made you happy today.

What's Your Mood?

How are you feeling today? Sad? Happy? Excited? Mad? Frustrated? Joyful?

Draw a self-portrait of how you feel today on the image below.

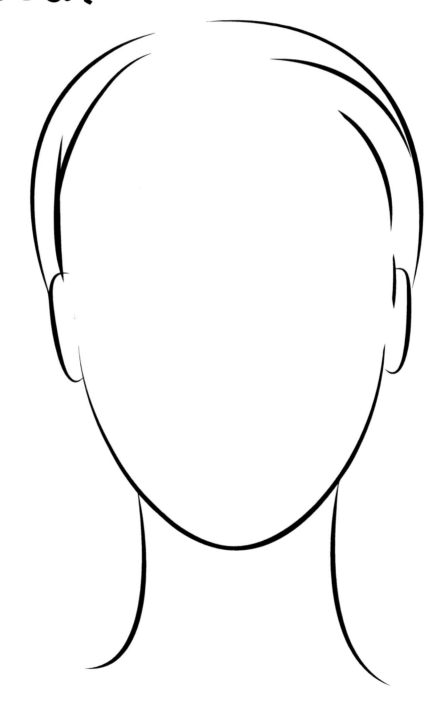

name: _____

Name: Date:

WHAT HAPPENED TODAY?

Write about something that frustrated you today.
What did you do about it?

MINDFUL MOVEMENT

Stand in place and count your heartbeat for one minute.
Run in place for one minute.
Count your heartbeat again.
Do you notice a difference?
Is your heart rate faster after you run in place?
How does that make you feel?
Where do you feel different in your body?

_____

_____

_____

_____

_____

_____

_____

_____

_____

Name: Date:

WHAT ARE YOU THANKFUL FOR TODAY?

Write about three things that you are thankful for today.

Name _____

Date _____

GROWING YOUR AWARENESS

During the daytime, find a quiet space outside or near a window. Take a few deep, cleansing breaths, close your eyes if you want, and bring awareness to your environment. Then, draw what you hear and smell. Come back to the same spot at night and draw what you hear and smell. Compare your drawings.
Write down things that are the same and things that are different.

DAY

NIGHT

SIMILARITIES

_____
_____
_____
_____
_____

DIFFERENCES

_____
_____
_____
_____
_____

Name: Date:

WHAT HAPPENED TODAY?

Write about something that happened today
that you would like you remember.

I am the source of my own happiness.

Set your intention

CHECK THREE THINGS YOU WILL DO THIS
WEEK TO BE MORE MINDFUL.
BE INTENTIONAL.

- [ ] DRINK 8 GLASSES OF WATER A DAY
- [ ] UNPLUG FROM SOCIAL MEDIA AND VIDEO GAMES FOR 24 HOURS
- [ ] SIT IN THE SUNSHINE
- [ ] TAKE A WALK
- [ ] CREATE A GRATITUDE JAR
- [ ] 3 MINUTES OF BELLY BREATHING
- [ ] TAKE A DANCE BREAK
- [ ] LISTEN TO YOUR FAVORITE SONG
- [ ] CALL A FRIEND
- [ ] VISIT A FAMILY MEMBER
- [ ] TAKE A BIKE RIDE
- [ ] TAKE A WARM BATH
- [ ] CUDDLE A PET
- [ ] TRY SOMETHING NEW
- [ ] READ A GOOD BOOK

Chicken Breath
Dynamic breathing
(3 minutes)

CHICKEN BREATH LOOKS RIDICULOUS, SO DON'T BE AFRAID TO LOOK SILLY! MAKE SURE YOU KEEP YOUR MOUTH CLOSED DURING THIS ACTIVITY, SO YOU WON'T BECOME DIZZY. THIS PRACTICE IS GREAT WHEN YOU NEED A QUICK BURST OF ENERGY.

STEPS

1. STAND UP AND STRETCH.
2. BEGIN TO TAKE VERY QUICK, SHORT, DEEP BREATHS IN RAPID SUCCESSION.
3. BEND YOUR ARMS AND PUMP THEM UP AND DOWN (LIKE A BELLOW) WHILE YOU BREATHE. YOUR ARMS SHOULD LOOK LIKE WINGS, BUT THEY SHOULDN'T BE LOOSE OR FLAPPY. THEY SHOULD BE STRONG.
4. YOUR ARMS SHOULD PUMP UP AS YOU INHALE AND SHOULD PUMP DOWN AS YOU EXHALE.
5. BEGIN TO BEND YOUR KNEES AS YOU EXHALE AND STRAIGHTEN YOUR KNEES AS YOU INHALE.
6. AFTER TWO MINUTES, STOP, CLOSE YOUR EYES, AND DRAW YOUR ATTENTION BACK TO YOUR BREATH.

HOW DOES YOUR BODY FEEL?

Name: _____   Date: _____

WHAT
HAPPENED
THIS WEEK

Draw a picture of something you want to remember from each day.

sunday

monday

tuesday

wednesday

thursday

friday

saturday

Write a few sentences explaining why you picked those moments to remember.

_____

_____

MINDFUL MOVEMENT

Create your own dance or yoga sequence and describe it below.

WHAT HAPPENED TODAY?

Write about something that frustrated you today.
What did you do about it?

WHAT ARE YOU THANKFUL FOR TODAY?

Write about three things that you are thankful for today.

GROWING YOUR AWARENESS

During the daytime, find a quiet space outside or near a window. Take a few deep, cleansing breaths, close your eyes if you want, and bring awareness to your environment. Then, draw what you hear and smell. Come back to the same spot at night and draw what you hear and smell. Compare your drawings. Write down things that are the same and things that are different.

Day	Night

⭐ ⭐ **SIMILARITIES** ⭐ ⭐

_____

_____

_____

⭐ ⭐ **DIFFERENCES** ⭐ ⭐

_____

_____

_____

Name: Date:

WHAT HAPPENED TODAY?

Write about something that happened today
that you would like you remember.

You are more than enough.

You are one of a

kind...